I am wherever you are

In the light of loss,
paintings by N. A. Noël

This book
is dedicated
to those who weep
for lost loved ones.
Through paintings
inspired by color and light,
it has been created
to touch your heart.
Our hope is
to bring freedom
from your sorrow and
peace for your spirit.

They whom we love and lose
are no longer where they were before.
They are now...
wherever we are.

- Saint John Chrysostom

The great wonder
of the universe is this:

I am peace and joy

I am love and faith

I am wisdom and hope and truth.

I am body and spirit

And the mind of God.

In your deepest heart of hearts you know

I am.

- B. Milleson James

Wonderful spirit of heavenly life,
all the peace of the universe
is in your wistful gaze.
You bring to us a new awareness
of God in you,
And, therefore, of God in me.

- B. Milleson James

It lies around us like a cloud ~
A world we do not see;
Yet the sweet closing of an eye
May bring us there to be.

Its gentle breezes fan our cheek;
Amid our worldly care
Its gentle voices whisper love,
And mingle with our prayers.

Sweet hearts around us throb and beat,
sweet helping hands are stirred,
And palpitates the veil between
With breathings almost heard.

So thin, so soft, so sweet they glide,
So near to press they seem,
They seem to lull us to our rest,
And melt into our dream.

- Harriet Beecher Stowe

The sweet angels
take us to peace
never fear
quietly
lovingly
the angels come

- Marshall Stewart Ball

Do not stand
by my grave and weep
For I am not there, I do not sleep.
I am a thousand winds that blow
I am the diamond's glint on snow
I am the sunlight on ripened grain
I am the gentle autumn's rain
When you awaken in a morning hush
I am the swift uplifting rush
of quiet birds in circle flight.
I am the soft stars that shine at night
Do not stand at my grave and cry,
I am not there,
I did not die.

- Unknown

Tiny, sleepy Angel,
fresh from God, to God returned,
Perfection unaware,
You are most beloved, on Earth and Heaven:

Awaken now to joy.

- B. Milleson James

Beyond these chilling winds and gloomy skies
Beyond death's cloudy portal,
There is a land where beauty never dies ~
Where love becomes immortal.

- Nancy Priest Wakefield

In the dark, the I begins to see.

Your joy is your sorrow unmasked.
And the selfsame well from which your laughter rises
was often times filled with your tears.
And how else can it be?
The deeper that sorrow carves into your being,
the more joy you can contain.
Is not the cup that holds your wine
the very cup that was burned in the potter's oven?
And is not the lute that soothes your spirit,
the very wood that was hollowed with knives?
When you are joyous, look deep into your heart
and you shall find it is only that which has given you sorrow
that is giving you joy.
When you are sorrowful look again in your heart,
and you shall see that in truth
you are weeping for that which has been your delight.

- Kahlil Gibran

It is not always ours to understand
why morning passes to midnight
without full chance of day.
But in the darkest hours,
the light you were given,
however briefly,
will shine above you...
in the stars
and in the eyes
of an
angel.

- P. S. Points

I can tell you this
about Angel Children,
from my heart, where I know its truth:

In the hand of God,
or at His right side,
or on the cobbled, golden streets of Heaven,
His winged Angel Children
surpass in love and joy
all that they ever knew with us,
And lose forever
the merest memory of pain.

- B. Milleson James

In your eyes,
in the very first moment,
I could see the promise of God,
And I will remember forever
the peace that I saw there.
Surely you have brought
love and joy to Heaven as once
you brought them to Earth.

- B. Milleson James

The time may be delayed,
the manner may be unexpected,
but the answer is sure to come.
Not a tear of sacred sorrow,
not a breath of holy desire,
poured out to God will ever be lost,
but in God's own time and way
will be wafted back again in clouds of mercy,
and fall in showers of blessings on you,
and on those for whom you pray.

- Saint Thérèse

You are not alone, little soul,
Not here, not now,
Not before, not after.
We are all one, through all time:
Ourselves
And something greater than ourselves.
Always the same,
Always the one,
Always the love you knew, and were,
And still are.

- B. Milleson James

Long, long be my heart
with such memories filled!

Like the vase in which roses
have once been distilled ~

You may break, you may shatter
the vase if you will,

But the scent of the roses
will hang round still.

- Thomas Moore

Dear God,

I have lost my precious love.
I feel as though
my spirit is broken.

Please lift my heart
above this pain
to embrace your peace.

Reveal to me the truth
and show me that
love never dies.

Amen.

- Marianne Williamson

...Then steal away, give little warning,
Choose thine own time;
Say not good night, ~
but in some brighter clime
Bid me good morning.

- Anna Letitia Barbauld

Good night,
sweet prince:
And flights of angels
sing thee to thy rest...

- William Shakespeare

I AM WHEREVER YOU ARE

Some of the original paintings in this book are available as open-edition and/or limited-edition
fine art prints. For information on purchasing prints, award-winning books or
a free NOËL STUDIO color catalog:
1-800-444-6635
www.nanoel.com

Copyright © 2000 NOËL STUDIO, Inc.
5618 West 73rd Street
Indianapolis, IN 46278

Cover design by Betsy Knotts

ISBN 0-9652531-4-7

From THE PROPHET by Kahlil Gibran
Copyright 1923 by Kahlil Gibran and renewed 1951 by Administrators CTA of Kahlil Gibran Estate and Mary G. Gibran.
Reprinted by permission of Alfred A. Knopf, a Division of Random House Inc.
Canadian Distribution was granted by Gibran National Committee,
address: P.O. Box 116-5487, Beirut, Lebanon; fax (+961-1)396916; email: k.gibran@cyberia.net.lb

With Gratitude

To all those who shared with me their sorrow and faith,
this book is because of you.

With special thanks to:
B. Milleson James, for her wisdom and her words
Betsy Knotts whose talent for design helped bring this book together
Marshall Stewart Ball, for his divine message
P. S. Points for her prose
Marianne Williamson for her prayer

❧

Saint John Chrysostom
Harriet Beecher Stowe
Nancy Priest Wakefield
Kahlil Gibran
Saint Theresa
Thomas Moore
Anna Letitia Barbauld
William Shakespeare
...whose spirit continues to inspire us.

To Alexander and Michael
in memory of H.J. and Jack